MW00452113

Sound at Sight

2nd series

Sight reading for Singing

Book 3

Grades 6-8

Published by
Trinity College London Press
trinitycollege.com

Registered in England
Company no. 09726123

Copyright © 2014 Trinity College London

Second impression, March 2017

Unauthorised photocopying is illegal
No part of this publication may be copied or reproduced in any form or
by any means without the prior permission of the publisher.

Printed in England by Caligraving Ltd.

Sound at sight

Singing or playing music that has not been seen before is a necessary part of any musician's life, and the exploration of a new piece should be an enjoyable and stimulating process.

Reading music requires two main things: first, the ability to understand music notation on the page; second, the ability to convert what is seen into sound and perform the piece. This involves imagining the sound of the music before playing or singing it. This in turn implies familiarity with intervals, rhythmic patterns, textures and dynamics. The material in this series will help singers develop their skills and build confidence.

Trinity College London's sight reading requirements are stepped progressively between Initial and Grade 8, with manageable increases in difficulty between each grade. Some tips on exam preparation are given at the back of the book. In all cases, however, references to exam tests are avoided until *after* the relevant material has been practised. This is deliberate: many pupils find the prospect of being tested on sight reading skills to be quite inhibiting at first. The aim is to perform new pieces – the fact that they may be exam tests as well is far less important.

Acknowledgements

Thanks are due to the many composers who have contributed to the series: Robin Bigwood, James Burden, Humphrey Clucas, Colin Cowles, David Dawson, Sébastien Dédis, Peter Fribbins, David Gaukroger, Robin Hagues, Amy Harris, Chris Lawry, Peter Lawson, Jonathan Paxman, Danielle Perrett, Michael Zev Gordon.

Thanks are also due to Luise Horrocks, Geraint John, Harold Jones, Joanna Leslie, Anne Smillie and Eric Tebbett for their technical advice.

Special note

 It is not necessary for singers and their accompanists to buy two copies of this book. Accompanists may make one photocopy of any of the pages in this book. The copy will need to be reduced to 91% to fit on an A4 page.

Contents

Introduction

It is essential that you start with a good foundation in aural training. Make sure that you are thoroughly at home with pitching intervals both up and down from any note of the scale, major and minor. (Trinity's *Vocal Exercises Book 1* will help with this.) Singing is not about individual intervals - it is about intervals in context. Get to know what it feels like to sing a sixth from each note within a scale, for example: notice how some are major and some are minor sixths. Then choose one type (either major or minor sixth) and sing absolute intervals from each note of the scale, noticing this time how the notes that are outside the key 'feel' in the voice.

Notes of the tonic chord can help if you are not certain about the sound of any of the intervals. Remember: each note is no more than one step away from a note of the tonic chord. A note may be repeated with other notes in between: think back to the reference note in order to keep on course. Another thing to look for in melodies at this level is modulation. Try to notice if the modulation is going to a sharper/higher key (dominant, relative major, supertonic etc) or a flatter/lower one (subdominant, relative minor etc). Try to hear the sound of the new tonic in your head each time the music changes key.

Here are a few tips that you should bear in mind:

▶ rising melodies tend to go flat. Aim for wide semitones, tones and major thirds especially

▶ falling melodies can also go flat. Aim for small semitones and minor thirds especially

▶ repeated notes can easily slip a little. Listen carefully, and 'think up' the repeated notes so that they remain in the centre of the pitch

▶ if the melody returns to a note with others in between, listen carefully to make sure that you do return to exactly the same pitch. Once again, 'think up' this pitch especially after lower notes have intervened.

Try the pitching exercises in Trinity's *Vocal Exercises Book 2* (high or low edition). It is worth memorising these and repeating them often. Always practise pitching exercises with full attention.

Most vocal music has words. As in Books 1 and 2, the exercises in this book do not. Although this may seem artificial, it helps you to concentrate on the notes. It is suggested that you sing on [ɑ] or [ɪ] and use a light consonant on repeated notes and the first note of slurred groups. Either [l] or [d] will work well. You can also use sol-fa names or any other vowel sounds, with or without consonants, if you prefer.

Each exercise in this book is presented in high and low treble clef, and bass clef transpositions ie:

1a = high treble clef

1b = low treble clef

1c = bass clef

Grade 6

In these exercises you will develop even pace and fluency, rhythmic accuracy and effective phrasing.
Try to observe the dynamics and as much detail as possible.

1a

Track 1

1b

1c

Track 55

2a

Track 2

2b

Track 29

2c

3a

Track 3

3b

Track 30

3c

Track 57

4a

Track 4

 Grade 6

4b

 Track 31

4c

5a

Track 5

5b

5c

6a

6b

Track 33

6c

7a

7b

Track 34

7c

8a

8b

8c

Track 62

9a

Track 9

9b

Track 36

9c

Track 63

Grade 7

As pieces become longer, there should be increased understanding of the whole shape of the piece and how smaller phrases build to make the larger shape. Recognising and reproducing an appropriate style is important: use different colours depending on the style. Chromaticism will also become more common now.

10a

Track 10

10b

Track 37

10c

Track 64

11a

Track 11

11b

11c

Track 65

12a

12b

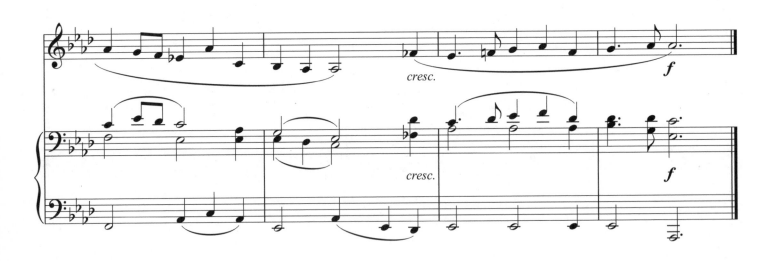

12c

13a

Track 13

13b

13c

14a

14b

Track 41

14c

Track 68

15a

Track 15

15b

Track 42

15c

Track 69

16a

16b

16c

17a

Track 17

17b

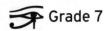

17c

18a

18b

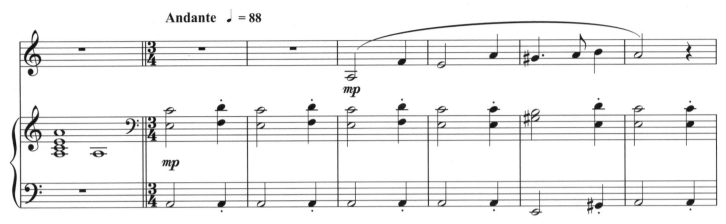

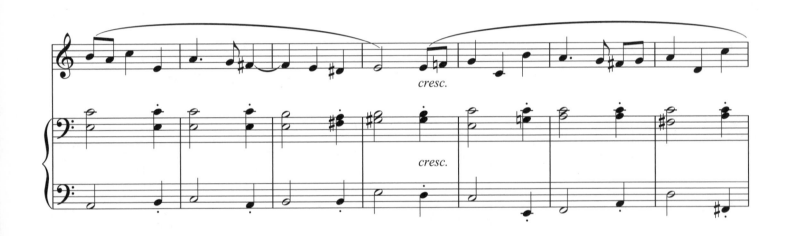

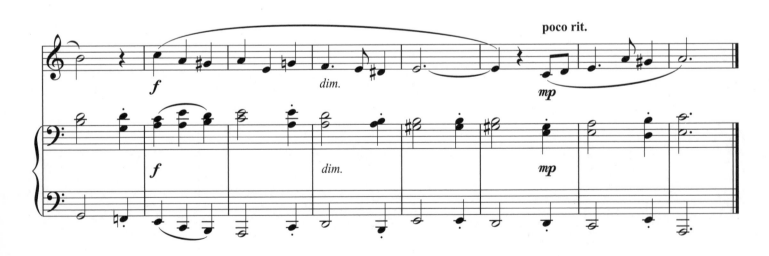

18c

Grade 8

You will now be required to sing in an even wider variety of keys and styles. As the melodies become longer, you need to think carefully about phrasing and the overall shape of each piece. There will be more detail to take in, with more variety in articulation and dynamics to include while maintaining the flow of the music. Rhythmic elements become increasingly important in defining the character of pieces.

19a

Track 19

58

19b

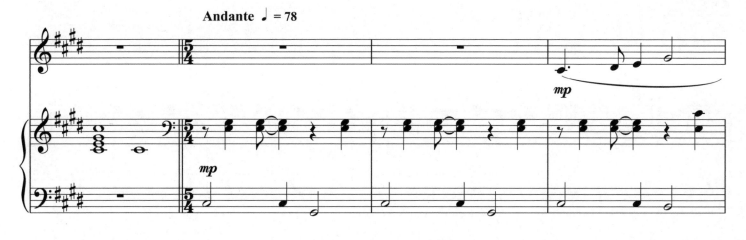

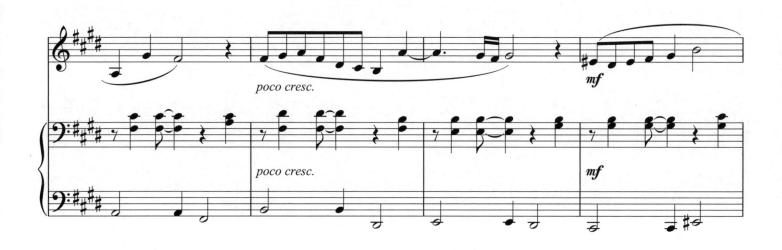

19c

20a

Track 20

20b

Track 47

20c

21a

21b

21c

22a

22b

Track 49

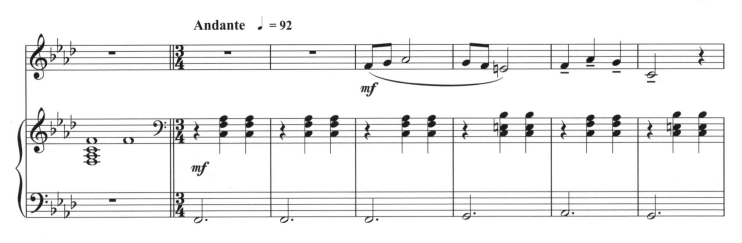

22c

23a

Track 23

23b

23c

24a

24b

Track 51

24c

25a

25b

25c

Track 79

26a

26b

Track 53

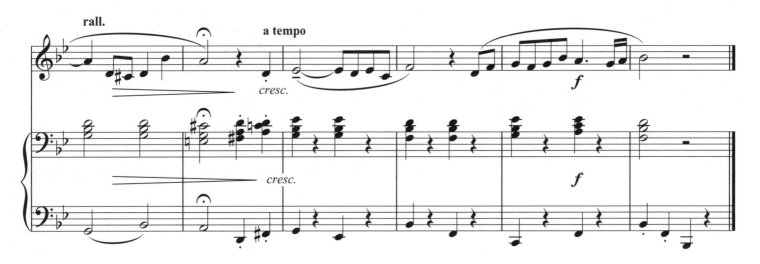

26c

Track 80

27a

Track 27

27b

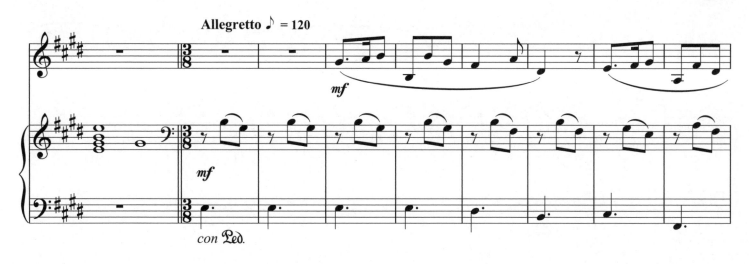

27c

Track 81

Exam advice

In an exam, you have half a minute to prepare your performance. Use this time wisely:

▶ Check the key and time signature. You might want to remind yourself where the semitones occur, checking for signs of major or minor first.

▶ Look for any accidentals, particularly when they apply to more than one note in the bar.

▶ Plan your breathing and any large intervals or changes of key.

▶ Set the pace in your head and read through the piece, imagining the sound. It might help to clap or tap the rhythm. You can also try out any part of the test if you want to.

▶ Have you imagined the effect of the dynamics?

When the examiner asks you to sing the piece, sing it at the pace set by the introduction. Fluency is more important than anything else: make sure that you keep going whatever happens. If you make a little slip, do not go back and change it. Give a performance of the piece: if you can sing the pieces in this book you will be well-prepared, so enjoy the opportunity to sing music that you didn't know beforehand.

Sight reading requirements at a glance

The following table gives a general guide to the requirements singers can expect to encounter at each level, and where they are encountered in this series of books. The complete detailed specifications can be found in the current syllabus. **Candidates should always refer to the requirements listed in the most recent syllabus when preparing for an exam.**

Grade	Time signatures (cumulative*)	Note values (cumulative*)	Dynamics & tempi (cumulative*)	Articulation (cumulative*)	Key & range (cumulative*)	Other (cumulative*)
Initial	$\frac{2}{4}$	♩ and 𝅗𝅥	*moderato*, ***mf***		C major; major/minor 6th	by step and major triad only
Grade 1	$\frac{4}{4}$	𝅝 and 𝄻		*legato*, simple phrasing (using breath marks *or* slurs)	G major; minor 7th	small intervals including leaps to dominant above and below
Grade 2	$\frac{3}{4}$	𝅗𝅥. and ties	*allegretto*		A minor	
Grade 3		♪, 𝄾 and 𝄼	*andante*		F major; D melodic minor; octave	leaps of a sixth
Grade 4		𝅘𝅥. and 𝄿	***p*** , ***f*** , *dim.* and *cresc.*		D and B♭ major; E minor	some chromatic notes
Grade 5	$\frac{6}{8}$	♪, 𝄿 and dotted notes	*rall., accel., a tempo,* pause		A and E♭ major; B and G minor; major/minor 9th	modulation; leaps of a seventh *or* an octave
Grade 6	$\frac{3}{8}$				F♯ and C minor	progressive introduction of chromatic intervals
Grade 7	$\frac{9}{8}$	triplets	any common terms and signs		E and A♭ major; C♯ and F minor; major/minor 10th	
Grade 8	$\frac{2}{2}, \frac{5}{4}$ and changing time signatures	duplets			B and D♭ major; G♯ and B♭ minor (incl. double sharps and flats)	

This book (Grade 6, Grade 7, Grade 8)

* Tests may also include requirements from preceding grades.